DK BIG BOOK OF
RACING CARS

Trevor Lord

A Dorling Kindersley Book

LONDON, NEW YORK, MUNICH,
PARIS, MELBOURNE, AND DELHI

Senior Editor   Shaila Awan
Senior Art Editor   Susan St. Louis

Art Director   Mark Richards
Jacket Designer   Victoria Harvey
DTP Designer   Louise Paddick
Picture Researcher Angela Anderson
Production   Melanie Dowland
Photography   Richard Leeney

First published in Great Britain in 2001
This edition published 2007
by Dorling Kindersley Limited
80 Strand
London WC2R 0RL
A Penguin Company

2 4 6 8 10 9 7 5 3 1

Copyright © 2001 Dorling Kindersley Limited, London

A CIP catalogue record for this book
is available from the British Library.

ISBN: 978-0-7513-3521-7
bookcode = KD 001

Colour reproduction by GRB Editrice of Italy
Printed and bound in Singapore by Tien Wah Press

Dorling Kindersley would like to thank:
Anderson CSK Motorsport; ATV World;
David Atkins at Atkins Racing Limited;
Audi Sport Press, Germany and UK; Greg Bringel;
Greg Foley; GSE Racing; Hendrick Motorsports;
Dean Hovey; Jaguar Cars Limited; Bruce Mullins;
Patrick Racing; Subaru World Rally Team.

The publisher would like to thank the following for their
kind permission to reproduce their photographs:

a=above, c=centre, b=below, l=left, r=right, t=top

Neil Bruce/Peter Roberts Collection: Neil Bruce 31t;
Hulton Getty: 30tl; Lat Photographic: 4tl;
National Motor Museum, Beaulieu: 30-31c;
Indianapolis Motor Speedway 1998 Copyright
Indianapolis: 31c; Double Red 12tl.

see our complete
catalogue at
www.dk.com

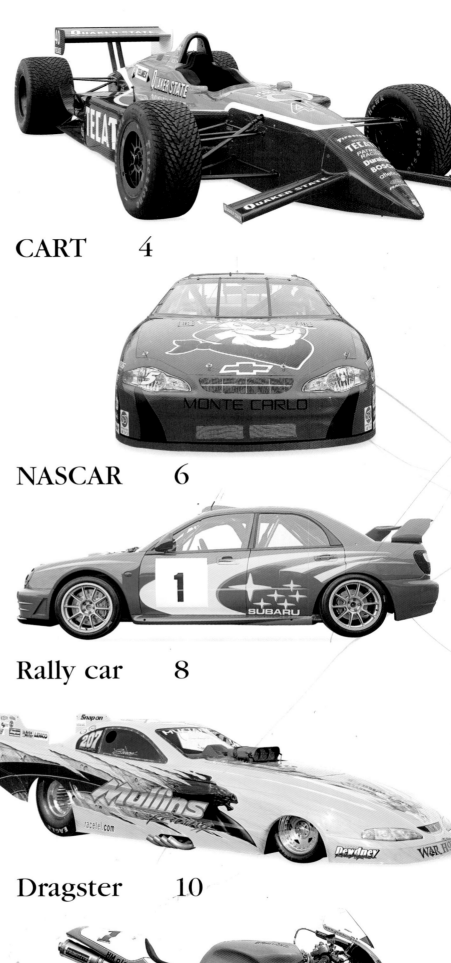

CART   4

NASCAR   6

Rally car   8

Dragster   10

Superbike   12

Snowmobile   14

Enduro bike   24

Quad   16

Formula One   18

Sports car   26

Kart   20

Baja buggy   28

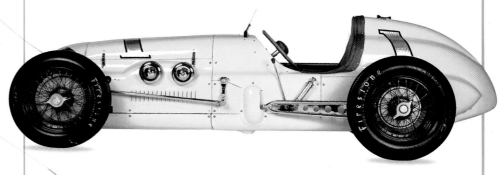

Classic racing cars   30

Racing truck   22

Glossary and Index   32

CART

CART (Championship Auto Racing Teams) was set up in the USA to organize races on street circuits, racetracks, and banked ovals. The same cars and drivers race at all three types of track, so the drivers have to be more versatile than those racing in Formula One. The season, which lasts 10 months, takes the teams all around the world.

Drivers racing this close together next to a concrete wall need great skill and a lot of courage.

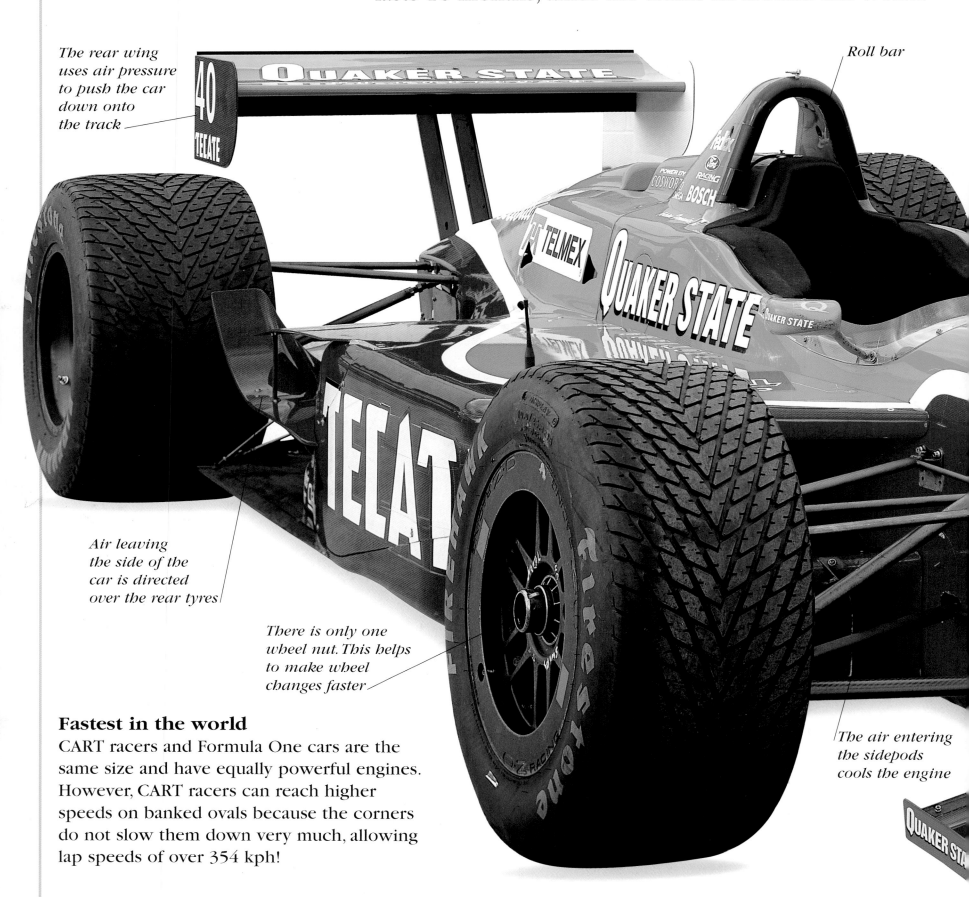

The rear wing uses air pressure to push the car down onto the track

Roll bar

Air leaving the side of the car is directed over the rear tyres

There is only one wheel nut. This helps to make wheel changes faster

The air entering the sidepods cools the engine

Fastest in the world

CART racers and Formula One cars are the same size and have equally powerful engines. However, CART racers can reach higher speeds on banked ovals because the corners do not slow them down very much, allowing lap speeds of over 354 kph!

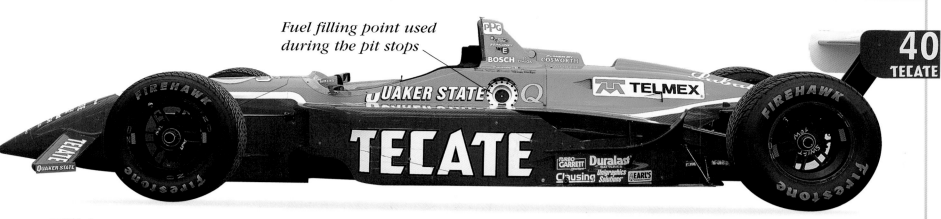

Fuel filling point used during the pit stops

Fill it up
With a fuel tank capacity of 159 litres, this car can only race for about 207 kilometres. To continue the race, the driver has to make a pit stop and refuel.

Ready for rain
These tyres have tread. They are used when the car is raced on a wet track and are called "wets". The tyres used on a dry track are completely smooth and they are known as "slicks".

The mirror allows the driver to watch the cars behind

This panel can be removed to adjust the suspension

This rod is moved by the steering wheel to help steer the car

The nose cone can be changed very quickly in the pits if it gets damaged

The front wings push down, balancing the rear wing

One of the rules for stock car racing is that the cars must only have one seat.

NASCAR

NASCAR takes its name from the National Association of Stock Car Auto Racing. The first races were held over 50 years ago in Daytona, Florida in the USA. Part of the track in those days was on the beach, so the races had to be timed to fit in with the tides. A lot has changed since then!

A real racing car

This stock car may look like a Chevrolet Monte Carlo, but it is not! All the cars competing in NASCAR events are proper racing cars fitted with lightweight bodies, but made to look like production cars.

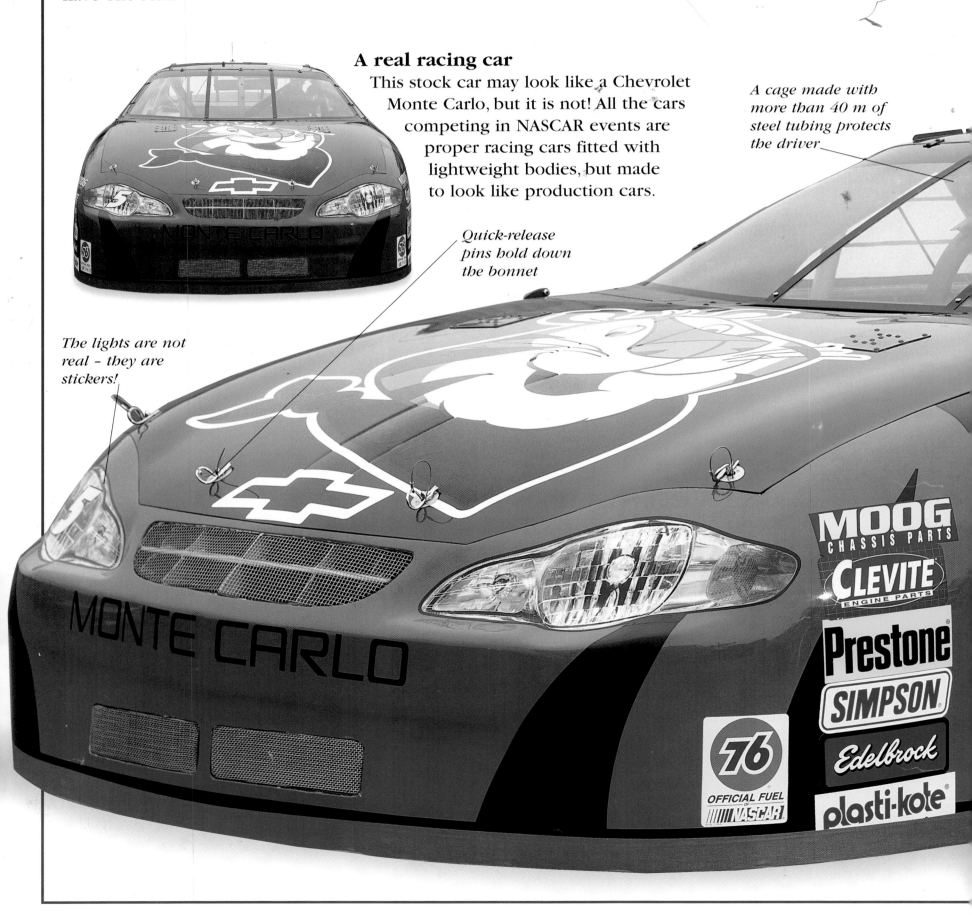

A cage made with more than 40 m of steel tubing protects the driver

Quick-release pins hold down the bonnet

The lights are not real – they are stickers!

MONTE CARLO

MOOG CHASSIS PARTS

CLEVITE ENGINE PARTS

Prestone

SIMPSON

Edelbrock

76 OFFICIAL FUEL OF NASCAR

plasti-kote

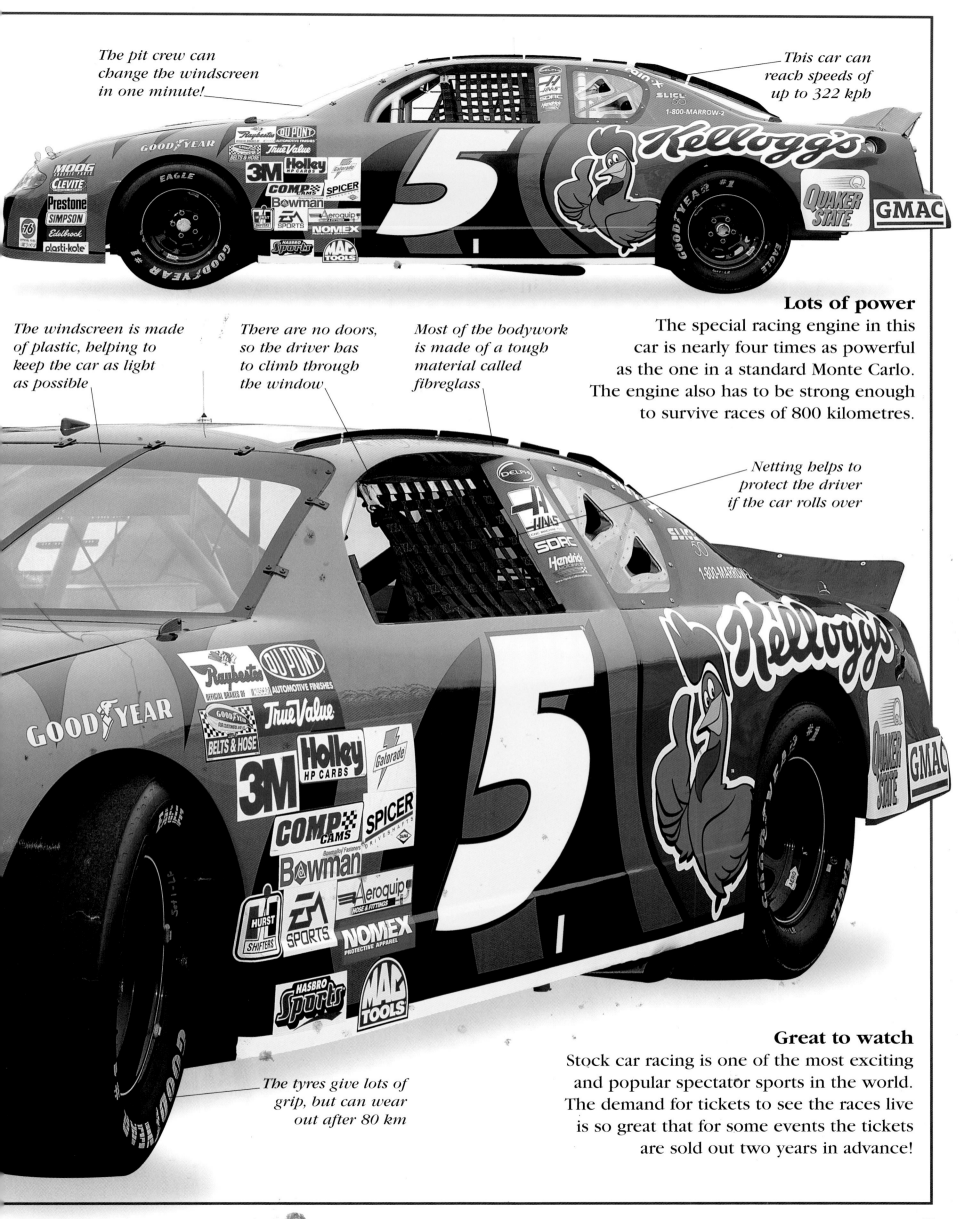

The pit crew can change the windscreen in one minute!

This car can reach speeds of up to 322 kph

The windscreen is made of plastic, helping to keep the car as light as possible

There are no doors, so the driver has to climb through the window

Most of the bodywork is made of a tough material called fibreglass

Lots of power

The special racing engine in this car is nearly four times as powerful as the one in a standard Monte Carlo. The engine also has to be strong enough to survive races of 800 kilometres.

Netting helps to protect the driver if the car rolls over

The tyres give lots of grip, but can wear out after 80 km

Great to watch

Stock car racing is one of the most exciting and popular spectator sports in the world. The demand for tickets to see the races live is so great that for some events the tickets are sold out two years in advance!

Rally car

Most racing vehicles are designed to perform well on a particular surface, such as tarmac or sand, but a rally car has to be far more versatile. A rally car has to be able to motor along snow-covered roads, pass through muddy forests, or go across deserts. With little more than a change of tyres, a rally car has to be fast and durable in all these conditions.

The navigator is responsible for telling the driver about the hazards that lie ahead.

The radio aerial enables the driver and navigator to keep in contact with the team

The rear wing helps to keep the car level when it flies through the air

Four-wheel drive
Most cars transmit power only to two wheels. But when a car is accelerating fast, or travelling on slippery surfaces, it needs a lot of grip from the tyres. So a rally car transmits power to all four wheels. This enables the car to travel at speed on some of the toughest tracks in the world.

The wheels are made of a strong, light material called magnesium

Ready for the road

Rally cars are fitted with indicators, number plates, and even a tax disc. This allows the cars to be driven on roads that are part of the racetrack.

Roll cage

A thin film of plastic covers the glass. This helps to hold the glass in place if the windscreen shatters

Quick change!

Time is set aside during a rally for the team mechanics to work on the car. The longest block of time is 40 minutes, but the Subaru mechanics are so fast that they can change a gearbox in 15 minutes!

The air intakes work even when the car is travelling sideways!

This front panel can be replaced by one with extra lights for rallying at night

9

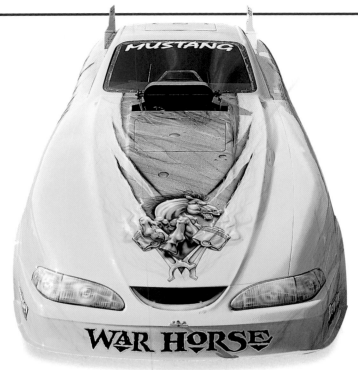

Dragster

In drag races, two cars race against each other in a straight line over a distance of 400 metres. The cars are more powerful than those used in any other type of motor sport. Drag racing started in the USA, but it is now popular all around the world.

Funny car!

"Funny cars" are dragsters that have lightweight bodies built to look like a standard production car. Of all the dragster classes fitted with full bodies, funny cars are the fastest and most spectacular.

The fins help to keep the dragster travelling in a straight line

The windows do not open, so these holes let in fresh air for the driver

This car uses 1,500 times as much fuel as a family car would need to cover 400 metres

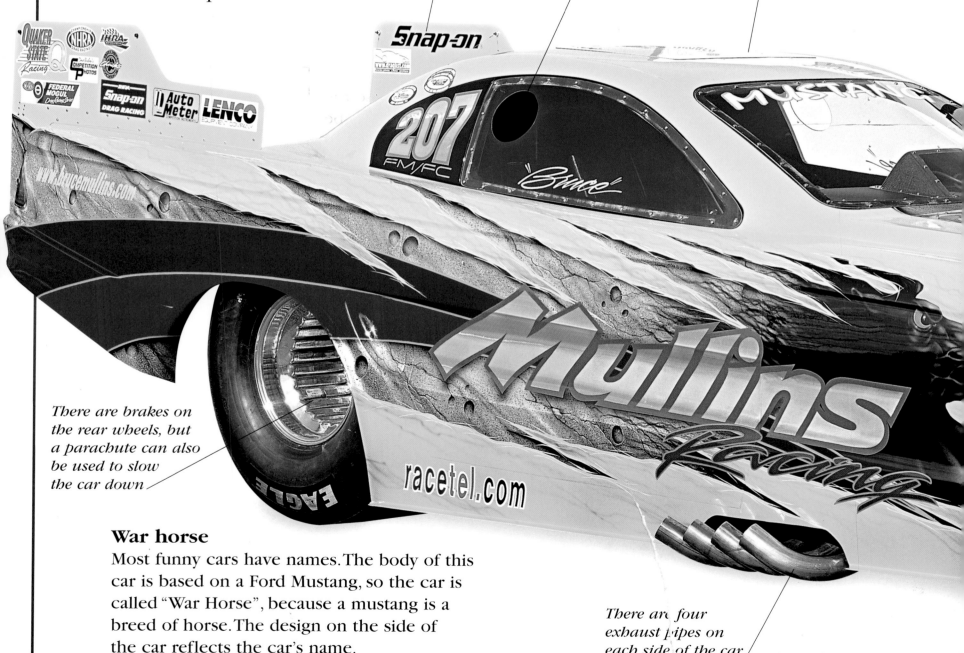

There are brakes on the rear wheels, but a parachute can also be used to slow the car down

War horse

Most funny cars have names. The body of this car is based on a Ford Mustang, so the car is called "War Horse", because a mustang is a breed of horse. The design on the side of the car reflects the car's name.

There are four exhaust pipes on each side of the car

This engine will take the car to 380 kph in less than 6 seconds!

For safety reasons, the fuel tank is positioned as far away from the driver as possible

The supercharger pushes air into the engine to make it more powerful

Nose in the air

The body of a funny car can be lifted clear of the engine, making it easier for the mechanics to work on the car. This is very important because the powerful engine has to be rebuilt with new parts after each race.

An on-board fire extinguisher is fitted in case of fire

There are no doors on a dragster, so the driver has to be seated and strapped in before the body is lowered.

Air intakes

The front wheels will lift clear of the ground at the start of a run

Superbike

Superbike races attract enormous crowds all around the world. One of the reasons for this popularity is that the bikes are based on the machines we see on the road every day. This does not mean they are slow – Superbikes can lap some racetracks as fast as 500cc Grand Prix bikes!

Superbike riders have special pads on their leather suits to allow their knees to slide along the track.

Much more than a road bike
Superbikes look like road bikes, but in fact nearly every part is different. Specially manufactured, very expensive racing components make the Superbike much faster than the road version.

The number 1 shows that this is the champion's bike

Through the air
A narrow bike will move through the air more easily than a wider one, so designers try to make their bikes as narrow as possible. The top Superbikes use very slim engines, and this helps the designers to minimize the width of the bike.

The powerful brakes can stop a bike travelling at 320 kph in just 8 seconds

The tank must be big enough to carry fuel for the whole race because there are no pit stops

The seat padding is very thin, but the rider only sits on it along the straights

Special racing silencers make the Superbike much louder than a road bike

Sprocket

These smooth tyres can only be used on dry tracks

How fast?
Even the fastest racing bikes will never achieve the lap times set by the best racing cars because cars go around corners much faster than bikes. But in a straight line, this bike is nearly as fast as a Formula One car and can reach speeds of up to 320 kph!

The rider operates the gear lever with his foot

The footrest is in this high position so that it does not touch the racetrack on corners

Snowmobile

Snowmobile racing is very popular in the USA and Canada, where the winters are cold. The races range from short sprints to 3,200-kilometre endurance events. The top machines can reach speeds of up to 210 kph, but there is a special class where the speed is restricted to just 16 kph, and these snowmobiles can be raced by four-year-olds!

Cross-country snowmobile races can last for several days. Each team has two riders, who share the task of completing the course.

Turning corners

The front skis steer the snowmobile, and the rider uses the handlebars to control the skis. He can also help to change the direction of the snowmobile by leaning from one side to another.

Halogen headlights help to improve poor visibility

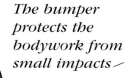

The bumper protects the bodywork from small impacts

Air vents are needed to cool the engine even when the races are in sub-zero temperatures

The skis on modern snowmobiles are made of plastic

Faster and faster

High performance snowmobiles are built to go fast, but like all racers, snowmobile riders want to go faster. To make this possible, the engines are modified to make them more powerful, the skis are changed to help cornering, and different suspension systems are tried to help the driver tackle uneven snow. The snowmobile may go faster, but for the rider it will never be fast enough!

Race clothing
has to give
protection and
be very warm

A crash helmet
is essential,
even in snow

The suspension
system is similar to
that of a racing car

The engine drives
this rubber track,
which digs into
the snow

The engine in a racing snowmobile
is as powerful as a Grand Prix
motorbike engine.

Quad

Quads are very much like motorbikes except for one obvious difference – they have four wheels! Many farmers use four-wheel drive quads to get around their farms, but the most exciting quads are the racing vehicles. These can accelerate as fast as Superbikes and reach speeds of up to 169 kph.

Quads can be raced on motocross racetracks or on ultra-fast tarmac tracks.

The modified engine is twice as powerful as the original engine

The bodywork is one of the few standard parts on this quad

A long swingarm is used to improve the stability of the quad

The engine is started using a kickstart

This bar helps to protect the rider's foot

There are extra wide wheel rims for the wide tyres

A very special quad

All quads made for racing are fast, but many riders modify their bikes to make them go even faster. Just about every part of this quad has been altered or replaced to make it longer, wider, lighter, and more powerful than it was before. The parts are very expensive, and a quad like this could cost 10 times as much as a standard one.

This racing quad is for children between 12 and 15 years old

A wide and light handlebar is used. This makes the racing quad easier to handle

Quads for children

The fun of quad bike racing is not restricted to adults since quads are made especially for children. The smallest quads can be ridden by six-year-olds, who move up to slightly larger bikes when they reach the age of 12. And at the age of 16, it is time to join the adults on full-size machines.

A large radiator helps to cool the powerful engine

A bumper bar protects the front of a quad in a collision

The quad uses very expensive racing suspension units

This tyre is designed to work on both dirt and tarmac

Long suspension links make the quad wider than a standard quad. This helps with cornering

Formula One

Formula One cars are the most advanced technically of all racing cars, and can reach speeds of up to 340 kph on a racetrack. The best drivers from all around the world compete in as many as 17 races in one season. The races take place in 16 countries across five continents. So the winner really deserves to be called the World Motor Racing Champion!

Built by hand

The Jaguar Formula One car starts its life as a drawing on a computer screen. It takes skilled mechanics up to nine months to fit the 3,500 individual parts that make up the race car!

No expense spared!

All the teams racing in Formula One build their own cars in specially designed workshops. Each car is made from very expensive materials that are both light and strong, such as titanium and carbon fibre. To design a car, buy the materials, and then build it costs several million pounds, and a team can need up to nine cars in one season!

Over 2,500 new tyres are taken to every Formula One race

The car's body is made of carbon fibre

Different front wings are fitted for long, fast tracks and short, twisty ones

The aerodynamic shape of the nose cone allows air to flow over the front wing

This is where the jack lifts the front of the car during the pit stops

BECK'S

TEXACO

LEAR

Front wing

Rear wing

There is an on-board camera on each car

On the track

Aeroplanes use wings to lift them into the air. Formula One cars also use wings, but they are turned over so that instead of lifting, the wings help to keep the car on the track.

The driver uses these paddles behind the steering wheel to change gear

During a race, the tyre gets very hot. This helps the car to grip the track

The bodywork is less than 4 cm above the track surface

This rod operates one of the very stiff suspension springs – Formula One cars are built for speed not comfort!

A race can be won or lost on a pit stop. So trained mechanics work at lightning speed to change the tyres and refuel in a matter of seconds!

19

Kart

The first karts were built in the USA over 40 years ago and were known as go-karts. They were powered by lawnmower engines and were raced around supermarket car parks. When faster karts were built, the racing was moved to purpose-built tracks, and the machines were called karts.

Kart racing takes place on full-size racetracks. The tracks can be nearly seven kilometres long.

The driver's seat is positioned to the side of the kart, helping to make room for the engine

Roll restraint

A small, extra wing on each side helps to keep the kart on the ground

A kart engine is similar to the engine used in a racing motorbike

The tyre is a smaller version of a racing car's tyre

The sidepod allows the air to flow easily along the side of the kart

How fast?

The fastest karts can reach 100 kph in less than 2.5 seconds. No road car in the world can accelerate this fast! Karts have a maximum speed of over 240 kph, and can go around tight and twisty corners faster than any other type of racing vehicle. As a result, karts can lap some circuits faster than 500cc Grand Prix motorbikes!

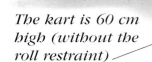

The kart is 60 cm high (without the roll restraint)

A bumpy ride

Karts have no springs for suspension. The tubular-steel frame does bend and flex a little, and the air-filled tyres help, but the driver still gets a very bumpy ride.

The driver changes gear with this lever

The position of the rear wing can be changed to suit different tracks

Sleek bodywork

To help achieve very high speeds on full-size racetracks, karts are fitted with aerodynamic bodywork. Air pressure on the bodywork also helps by pushing the kart down onto the track.

The washers are made of aluminium to help keep the kart as light as possible

Most of this bodywork is removed when the kart races on very short tracks

John Riley

Racing truck

The early racing trucks were similar to the ones we see on the road every day. But today, racing trucks are specially built for competition. A top racing truck weighs over five tonnes, which is the same as eight family cars! Despite this incredible weight, the trucks are not slow – they can accelerate from 0 to 100 kph as fast as a modern sports car!

Trucks racing this close together would probably make the ground shake!

The coupling for a trailer is fitted but never used

The air supply divides to deliver air to both sides of the engine

Racing springs

In the driving seat
Truck racing is just as competitive as any other type of motor sport, so for the top teams having a good driver is just as important as having a fast truck. Many championship-winning drivers have entered truck racing after successful careers in other sports, such as motorcycle and sports car racing.

Big and powerful engine
Heavy racing trucks achieve amazing acceleration because they have huge engines. A truck engine is four times the size of a Formula One engine and twice as powerful.

Speed limit
Trucks may accelerate very quickly, but they are all limited to a top speed of 160 kph by the racing rules. A device called a tachograph, fitted to each truck, records the speeds achieved during a race and so checks that the drivers do not exceed this limit.

Special racing seats are fitted

Switches on the small steering wheel enable the driver to change gear

Air hitting the windscreen is pushed up into this air scoop

Trucks are the tallest vehicles to be seen on racetracks. This one is 2.7 m high

Rear-view mirror

MercedesService Card

RECARO

Vanelius

8

Continental

Radiators keep the engine, gearbox, and brakes cool

There are no headlights on a racing truck

Enduro bike

Enduro racing can take place through forests or across deserts. The races can take just a few hours, or last for days. Some races even take weeks to complete! For the longer races, the riders have support teams to help them look after their bikes. At the end of each day, the race is stopped, and the teams set up camp for the night. Then the race starts again the following morning.

Enduro bikes only look this clean before the race starts!

Riding high

All enduro bikes are built so that the engine is high off the ground. This enables the engine to clear obstacles, such as rocks and fallen trees.

Special bikes

Although enduro bikes look like some road bikes, they are very different. To survive day after day on the tough courses, the bikes have to be very strong. They also need to be able to go through sand, water, or mud without being damaged. To help achieve this, all top enduro bikes are carefully built by hand.

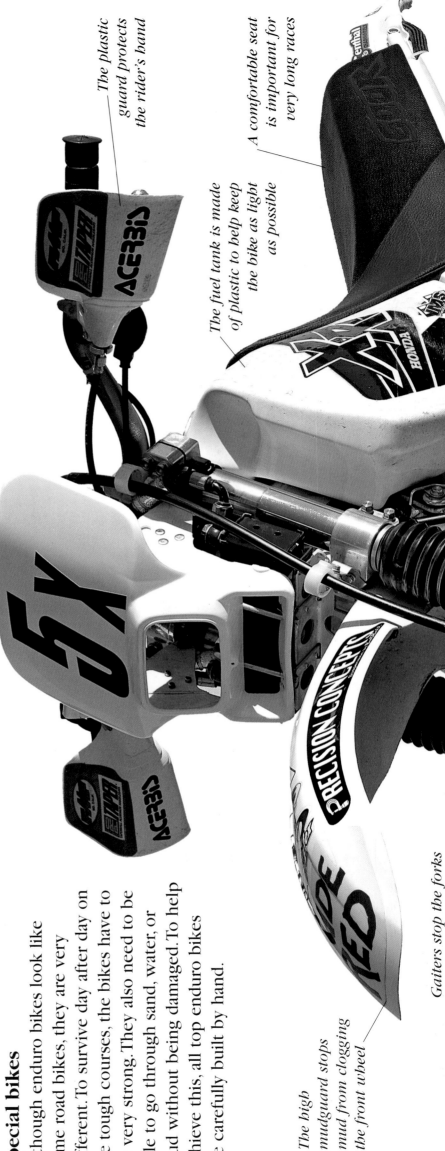

The plastic guard protects the rider's hand

A comfortable seat is important for very long races

The fuel tank is made of plastic to help keep the bike as light as possible

Gaiters stop the forks from being damaged

The high mudguard stops mud from clogging the front wheel

An extra steel tube gives greater protection to the engine

This guard stops the rider's hands or feet from being caught in the chain if there is a crash

Ridden at speed, the bikes take off into the air whenever they come to a small hill. This is very tiring for the riders, and only the fittest of them can complete the long enduro races.

The front brake is small because a large brake could cause the tyre to skid on loose surfaces

Each thin steel spoke may look weak, but is in fact very strong

The tyres are often filled with a jelly-like substance. This helps to prevent punctures

Long forks are needed to absorb the shocks when landing from high jumps

Sports car

Sports car races usually last for a very long time. The most famous of them all takes place at Le Mans, in France, and lasts for 24 hours. Each car in this race has a team of two or three drivers to share the driving. Between the start and the finish, the winning car will travel around 5,000 kilometres – the distance from England to the USA!

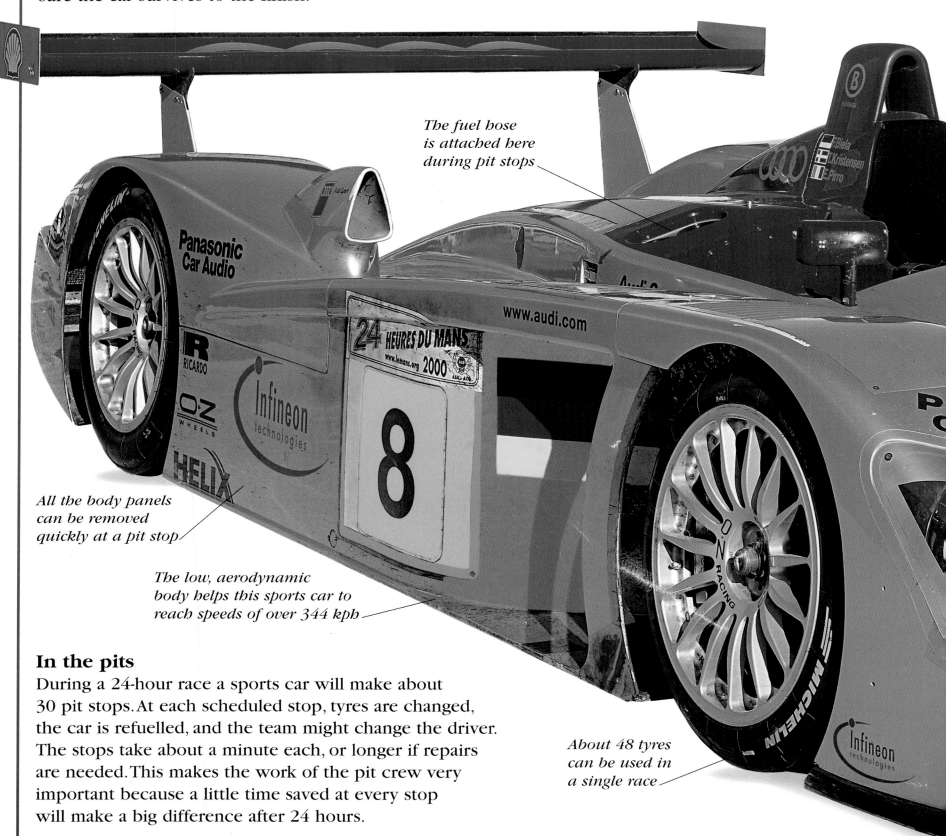

Whether it is day, night, dusk, or dawn, the drivers must drive as fast as they can. They must also drive carefully to make sure the car survives to the finish!

The fuel hose is attached here during pit stops

All the body panels can be removed quickly at a pit stop

The low, aerodynamic body helps this sports car to reach speeds of over 344 kph

About 48 tyres can be used in a single race

In the pits

During a 24-hour race a sports car will make about 30 pit stops. At each scheduled stop, tyres are changed, the car is refuelled, and the team might change the driver. The stops take about a minute each, or longer if repairs are needed. This makes the work of the pit crew very important because a little time saved at every stop will make a big difference after 24 hours.

Team colours

Many teams run more than one car in a race, and it is important that the cars can be identified easily. The Audi team's cars are all silver, but the red parts on this car are painted different colours on the other cars, so that the cars are easy to identify.

When the car is moving, air enters here to help cool the engine and brakes

The small screen helps to deflect the air over the driver's head

Room for two

Unlike Formula One or CART cars, the driver of a sports car does not sit in the middle of the car. This is because the rules state that there must be room for a passenger seat.

Powerful headlights are essential for night-time racing

A towing eye enables the car to be taken away if it breaks down or crashes

Baja buggy

Driving at high speed across rocks, boulders, and sand dunes often results in the cars taking off into the air.

The annual Baja 1000 is one of the world's toughest motor races. The drivers have to tackle nearly 1,600 kilometres of rough desert terrain at speeds of up to 193 kph. Other vehicles, such as pick-up trucks, quads, and bikes also compete. But the race is so tough that sometimes only a quarter of the starters make it to the finish.

Baja Buggy

To finish the Baja 1000, a car must be extremely strong. The best buggies are built around a cage made of steel tubing. This cage is strong enough to survive the many bumps and bangs it will face during the race. The strong frame also gives some protection to the driver and navigator if the car crashes.

The side nets help to keep the passenger's arms inside if the car rolls over

A high ground clearance enables the buggy to drive over rocks

The powerful lights are used for racing at night

Steel frame

Powerful engines

The engine in the back of a desert racing buggy needs lots of power to help it drive through deep sand and climb up the sides of mountains. The top desert racers have engines that are as powerful as those in Formula One or CART cars.

The dampers stop the car from bouncing on the springs

The long suspension springs help to keep the wheels on the ground over bumpy territory

The deep tread tyres give good grip in the sand

The wheels have to survive landings from thousands of jumps

Classic racing cars

The early racing cars first competed in city-to-city races.

The idea of using cars for racing is not a new one. In fact, cars were first used for racing before they were ever used for personal transport. Since those early days, motor racing has not only provided exciting entertainment, but has also helped to make the cars we use on the road today both safer and faster by developing new ideas on the racetrack. Disc brakes, aluminium wheels, and rear-view mirrors were all first used on racing cars.

Rear-view mirror

The yellow-and-black colour scheme gave this car the name "Wasp"

This pointed tail is an early attempt at streamlining

Even in 1911 pit stops were used to change tyres

The Type 35 was a two-seater racing car

Marmon Wasp

The Marmon Wasp won the first Indianapolis 500 race in 1911. The car is also famous for being probably the first car in the world to be fitted with a rear-view mirror.

The Bugatti Type 35 won the very first Monaco Grand Prix

Bugatti Type 35

The Bugatti Type 35 is one of the most successful cars in the history of motor racing. Around 400 were built, and between them they won nearly 2,000 races in the period 1924 to 1931! Many people have also described it as the most beautiful racing car ever made. It was also the first car in the world to be fitted with aluminium wheels.

The gear lever, like the handbrake, was placed outside so that the car could be as narrow as possible

Handbrake

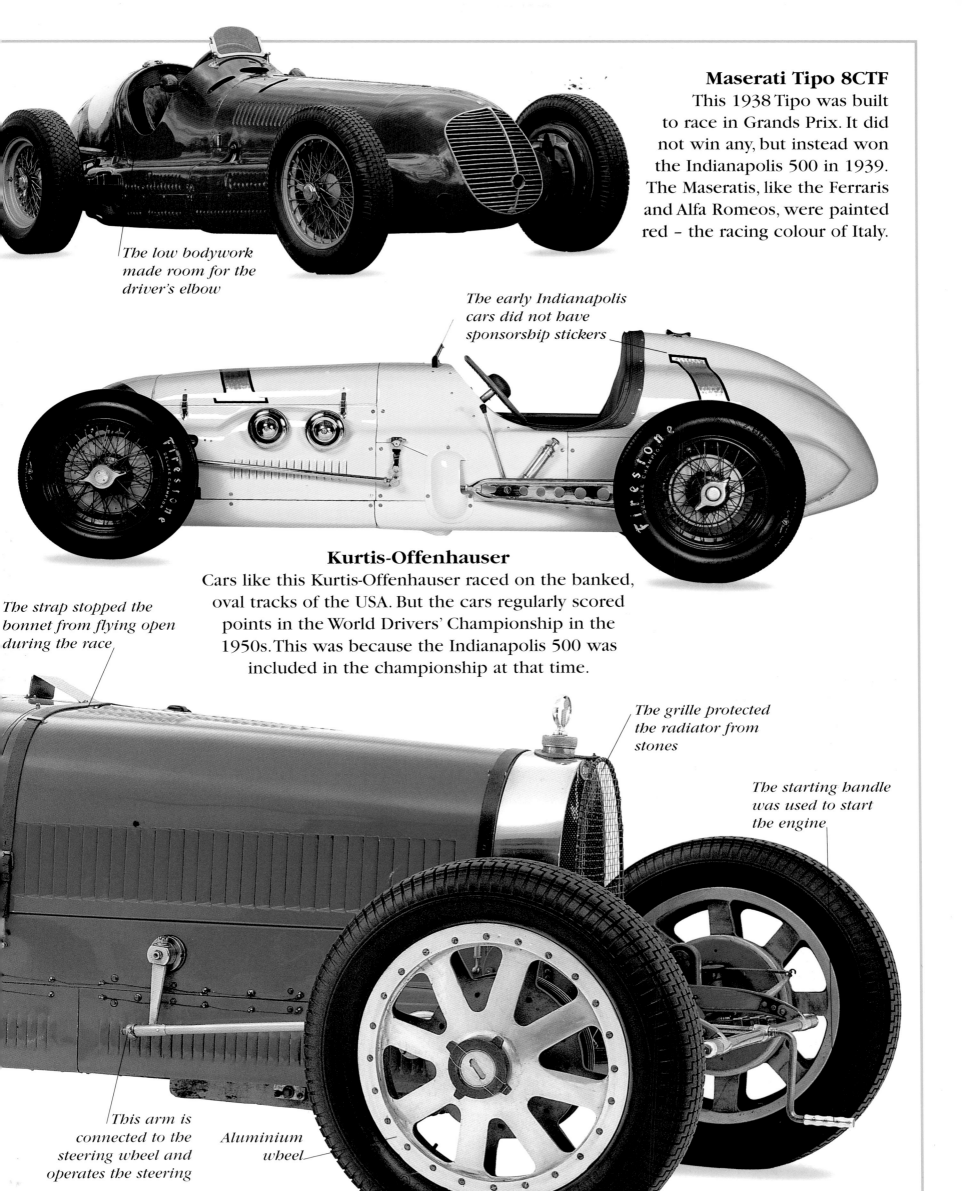

Maserati Tipo 8CTF
This 1938 Tipo was built to race in Grands Prix. It did not win any, but instead won the Indianapolis 500 in 1939. The Maseratis, like the Ferraris and Alfa Romeos, were painted red – the racing colour of Italy.

The low bodywork made room for the driver's elbow

The early Indianapolis cars did not have sponsorship stickers

Kurtis-Offenhauser
Cars like this Kurtis-Offenhauser raced on the banked, oval tracks of the USA. But the cars regularly scored points in the World Drivers' Championship in the 1950s. This was because the Indianapolis 500 was included in the championship at that time.

The strap stopped the bonnet from flying open during the race

The grille protected the radiator from stones

The starting handle was used to start the engine

This arm is connected to the steering wheel and operates the steering

Aluminium wheel

Glossary

Aerodynamic shape
A design that allows a vehicle to travel through the air easily.

Air intake
An opening in the bodywork that allows air to enter the vehicle.

Carbon fibre
A material similar to fibreglass but lighter and more expensive.

Damper
A device fitted to a vehicle's springs to stop it from bouncing.

Grand Prix
The name given to the races in both motorcycling and Formula One world championships. It is French for "big prize".

Indianapolis
The oval track in the USA where the annual 805-km race takes place.

Kickstart
A lever fitted to some quads and motorbikes. The lever is used to start the engine.

Le Mans
The French town that hosts the famous 24-hour car race.

Magnesium
A metal that is similar to aluminium but lighter.

Navigator
The person in a rally car who gives instructions, directions, and warnings to the driver.

Nose cone
The front part of the bodywork on a single-seater racing car.

Paddles
The levers fitted behind a steering wheel that are used for changing gear.

Pits
An area by the side of a racetrack. This area is used by teams to service their car during a race.

Radiator
To stop the engine from overheating, water is cooled by the radiator before it returns to the engine.

Sidepods
The bodywork on a single-seater racing car between the front and rear wheels.

Slicks
The name given to tyres without tread, which are used on dry racetracks.

Sprocket
The toothed wheel on a bike or quad that is driven by the chain.

Supercharger
A device that pushes air into an engine to make it more powerful.

Suspension springs
These springs are fitted to the wheels to make the ride more comfortable and to help keep the tyres in contact with the ground.

Titanium
A light and very expensive metal, which is sometimes used instead of steel.

Tread
The pattern on the surface of a tyre. This pattern helps the tyre to grip the track.

Wets
The name given to treaded tyres, which are used for racing in the rain.

Wings
Wings are fitted to the front and rear of some racing cars. They help to keep the car on the track.

Index

Aerodynamic 18, 21, 26
Alfa Romeos 31

Baja buggy 28-29
Bugatti Type 35 30-31

Carbon fibre 18
CART 4-5, 27, 29
Chevrolet Monte Carlo 6, 7
Classic racing cars 30-31

Dragster 10-11

Enduro bike 24-25

Ferraris 31
Ford Mustang 10
Formula One 4, 13, 18-19, 22, 27, 29
Four-wheel drive 8, 16
Funny cars 10-11

Go-karts 20

Kart 20-21
Kickstart 16
Kurtis-Offenhauser 31

Le Mans 26

Marmon Wasp 30
Maserati Tipo 8CTF 31
Magnesium 8

NASCAR 6-7
Navigator 8, 28
Nose cone 5, 18

Quad 16-17, 28

Racing truck 22-23
Rally car 8-9
Radiator 17, 23, 31

Snowmobile 14-15
Sports car 26-27
Sprocket 13
Superbike 12-13, 16
Supercharger 11

Tachograph 22
Titanium 18
Tread 5, 29

Wings 4, 5, 8, 18, 19, 20, 21